7-10

FASTEST

AND slowest

Written by
**Camilla
de la Bédoyère**

QEB

QEB Publishing

Designed and edited by Starry Dog Books Ltd
Picture research: Starry Dog Books Ltd

Consultant: Dr Gerald Legg,
Booth Museum of Natural History, Brighton

Copyright © QEB Publishing, Inc. 2010

Published in the United States by
QEB Publishing, Inc.
3 Wrigley, Suite A
Irvine, CA 92618

www.qed-publishing.co.uk

Library of Congress Cataloging-in-Publication Data
De la Bédoyère, Camilla.
  Fastest and slowest / Camilla de la Bédoyère.
    p. cm. -- (QEB Animal opposites)
  Includes index.
  ISBN 978-1-59566-760-1 (lib. bdg.)
  1. Animal locomotion--Juvenile literature. 2.
Physiology, Comparative--Juvenile literature. I. Title.
  QP301.D33 2011
  573.7'9--dc22

                              2010010663

ISBN 978 1 59566 760 1

Printed in China

Picture credits
Key: t = top, b = bottom, l = left, r = right, c = centre,
FC = front cover, BC = back cover.

A = Alamy, C = Corbis, D = Dreamstime.com,
FLPA = Frank Lane Picture Agency, G = Getty Images,
IQM = imagequestmarine.com, ISP = iStockphoto.com,
NPL = Nature Picture Library (naturepl.com),
PL = Photolibrary, PS = Photoshot, S = Shutterstock

FCt S/ © photobar, FCb S/ © Eric Isselée; BCtl, tr, bl
S/ © Picsfive, BCbr S/ © basel101658.

1l S/ © Dennis Donohue, 1r D/ © J20db; 2 S/ ©
Florian Andronache; 3t S/ © Steve Byland; 4-5 A/
© Mcmaster Studio, 4b S/ © originalpunkt; 5t S/ ©
Robin Keefe, 5b ISP/ © Andyworks; 6t S/ © D & K
Kucharscy, 6b PL/ © Joe McDonald; 7t A/ © Arco
Images GmbH, 7b S/ © orionmystery@flickr; 8t S/
© Sergey Kolodkin, 8b S/ © Florian Andronache;
9 NPL/ © Pete Oxford; 10l C/ © Visuals Unlimited,
10r C (Reuters)/ © Mick Tsikas; 10-11 NPL/ © Doug
Perrine, 11b D/ © Leyrer; 12l S/ © Mayskyphoto,
12-13 PL (OSF)/ © Daniel J. Cox; 13b NPL/ © Barry
Mansell; 14t IQM/ © Roger Steene, 14b S/ ©
Robyn Butler; 15t S/ © Tramper, 15b PL/ © Nigel
Dennis; 16c S/ © Mark Beckwith, 16b PL/ © Steve
Turner; 17 PL/ © John Hyde; 18t D/ © Joeyin, 18b
NPL/ © Tim MacMillan /John Downer Pro; 19t
S/ © worldswildlifewonders, 19b NPL/ © Nature
Production; 20t D/ © Gezafarkas, 20b NPL/ ©
Premaphotos; 21t PL/ © Paulo de Oliveira, 21b S/ ©
Vladimir Sazonov; 22c A/ © Premaphotos, 22b PL/
© Paul Freed; 23t PS/ © Martin Wendler, 23b PL/ ©
Donald Specker; 24 D/ © Mtrolle; 25t D/ © J20db,
25c S/ © Jefras, 25b S/ © EcoPrint; 26l IQM/ © Jez
Tryner, 26rPL/ © Keith Gillett; 27l PL/ © Marevision
Marevision, 27br S/ © Peter Leahy; 28bl S/ ©
Ingvars Birznieks, 28-29 NPL/ © Mark Carwardine;
29 bl © Killi Club Argentino, 29br G (Dorling
Kindersley Collection)/ © Jerry
Young; 32 S/ © Stephen Mcsweeny.

The words in **bold**
are explained in
the glossary on
page 30.

Contents

On the Move

All animals move. Some of them might move great distances, while others stay in one place and can move only parts of their bodies.

4

⇩ The long, moist part of a snail is actually its foot, not its body. The foot produces slime that helps protect it as it crawls over rough surfaces.

The way an animal moves from one place to another is called locomotion. Animals move to search for food, new **habitats,** and mates, and to escape from **predators**, rivals, or other dangers.

How do animals move?

Hummingbirds hover, snakes slither, and snails slip along on a trail of slime. Kangaroos jump, monkeys swing, sharks swim, and eagles soar through the sky. Animals can travel in many different ways— some fast, some slow.

ACTUAL «« SIZE »»

A duck's body is adapted to flying, walking, and swimming. Its foot is webbed, which means it can push water, forcing the duck forward as it swims.

Duck's webbed foot

in 1 2 3

⬇ *Wolves belong to the dog family. They have powerful muscles and strong bones, which help them to stalk prey, run fast, pounce, and fight.*

Fit for speed

The shape and size of an animal's body affect how it moves, and how fast it can go. Pronghorn deer are the fastest running animals on the planet over a long distance. Their huge lungs and big heart mean they can breathe very efficiently and provide power for their muscular legs.

A Need for Speed

Speed can be the key to survival for many animals. They move fast to catch their prey, or to avoid being caught themselves.

The fastest animals are more likely to survive, and therefore breed. The way that different types—or **species**—of animals change over time to become faster, bigger, or better is called evolution.

Run to safety

Most lizards can climb or walk on land, but basilisk lizards have developed a far more extraordinary way of getting about: they can run on water! Their long toes are webbed, which helps them to stay on the water's surface as they flee from predators across a river or pond.

The no. 1 fastest beetle **RECORD BREAKER** is the ...

TIGER BEETLE

Tiger beetles like this one chase their prey at top speed before grasping it in their strong jaws. The Australian tiger beetle is the world's fastest running **insect**, reaching speeds of 5.6 miles (9 kilometers) per hour.

⇐ A basilisk lizard holds its tail out behind it as it runs across the water. This helps it to keep its balance and stay dry.

6

↓ *Swifts swoop and glide through the air, catching insects as they go. Their legs and feet are so weak that they cannot perch.*

Swift in the air

Swifts are birds that are perfectly suited to life in the skies. They have become supreme fliers, able to make long journeys, called migrations, when they rarely land, and even sleep on the wing! Young birds may fly non-stop for over 300,000 miles (500,000 kilometers) before landing at their first nesting sites.

Jumping spiders may be small, but they have great eyesight and are super speedy! They use their eight eyes to find a victim, such as this wolf spider. Then they pounce, leaping up to 4 inches (10 centimeters) in one jump.

Jumping spider with wolf spider prey

ACTUAL
<<< SIZE >>>

in   1   2

Go Slow

Not all animals rely on speed for survival. Some of them prefer to "go slow."

Moving fast can attract unwanted attention. Moving slowly, or not at all, is a tactic that lots of animals use to stay alive.

Camouflage

Camouflaged animals have colors or markings that help them to blend in with their surroundings. Camouflage works best when an animal stays still. Stick insects are superb at doing this.

⇧ *A caterpillar stretches its body along a stem. Passing birds may mistake it for part of the plant.*

Praying mantis

6   5   4   3   2   1   in

Potoo

The potoo is a bird that spends all day motionless. It positions itself in a tree and **mimics** a branch. Staying still probably helps it to avoid being seen by predators. At night, it stirs itself into action and flits between branches, hunting for flying insects to eat.

⇨ *Potoos have bright yellow eyes, but they keep them shut during the day while they are pretending to be part of a tree.*

ACTUAL ««« SIZE »»»

A praying mantis ambushes its prey. It stays still, waiting for an insect, frog, or small bird to pass nearby. Then it launches its attack. Its leaflike wings provide camouflage, making it hard to spot among leaves.

Super Swimmers

Most speedy swimmers have evolved bodies that are perfectly shaped for moving through water.

Water is much denser—or thicker—than air, which means an animal needs lots of energy to move through it. A bullet-shaped body helps slice through the water.

Weak swimmers

Sea horses are slowpokes in water because they can scarcely bend their bodies to swim. These little fish are so weak that they have to wrap their tails around weeds to stop them from being carried away by **currents**.

The no. 1 fastest swimming bird **RECORD BREAKER** is the ...

GENTOO PENGUIN

Gentoo penguins are the fastest birds underwater. They can reach a top speed of 22 miles (36 kilometers) per hour in short bursts.

⇐ Sea horses cannot swim to escape predators, so they often use camouflage to hide. This one looks like part of the plant it is holding onto with its tail.

⇦ *Sailfish take their name from the large fins on their back. The fins help them to dash through the sea.*

ACTUAL ≪ SIZE ≫

Diving beetles swim using their hairy hind legs, which push water backward like oars. These insects carry bubbles of air underwater, so they can breathe.

Diving beetle

Flying undersea

An animal that is shaped to move through water is streamlined. The sailfish is one of the most streamlined of all swimmers. Its long, slender body is packed with **muscles**, which help it to reach a speed of 68 miles (109 kilometers) per hour. This makes it even faster than the fastest land animal, the cheetah.

1   2   3   4

Fast Fliers

There are only three groups of animals that can fly: birds, bats and insects.

Flying animals need wings. These limbs move air in such a way that an animal's body is lifted up and pushed forward.

Wingbeats

While the fastest little hummingbird can beat its wings at up to 90 beats per second, some birds scarcely have to move their wings at all. They travel great distances by gliding on hot air currents, called **thermals**.

⇐ *Hummingbirds can hover in front of a flower. They use their long bill and tongue to suck up sweet nectar from inside the flower.*

⬇ *Peregrine falcons are birds of prey, or hunting birds. They have good eyesight and sharp talons (claws), which they use to grab other birds to eat.*

King of speed

Peregrine falcons are not only the fastest fliers, they are the fastest of all animals. When they swoop downward, hunting smaller birds to eat, their dives can reach an eye-watering 124 miles (200 kilometers) per hour or more!

13

The no. 1 fastest flying bat **RECORD BREAKER** is the ...

BIG BROWN BAT

Bats are flying **mammals**. Their wings are made from a layer of skin stretched between their body and their fingers. The big brown bat flies faster than any other bat.

Digging Deep

Diggers and burrowers can find safety, and food, by moving around underground.

While some creatures can dig tunnels at speed, others take their time.

Rock-eaters

As sea urchins creep slowly over rocks, they graze on tiny animals and plants. They have tough teeth, as hard as stones, and their mouth is on their bottom. Sea urchins use their spines to burrow into sand. Some types eat their way through rocks to make tunnels. It can take them many years to dig the perfect hideout.

⇧ *This sea urchin lives in holes and under rocks. It moves very slowly and makes holes in rocks to hide.*

The no. 1 largest burrowing animal **RECORD BREAKER** is the ...

COMMON WOMBAT

Australian wombats are the largest burrowing animals. They can dig enormous underground **warrens**, with tunnels that extend for 650 feet (200 meters) or more.

Common mole

ACTUAL ‹‹‹ SIZE ›››

Moles use their strong front limbs like shovels. They have large claws for digging, and a small body that can squeeze through tunnels. One mole can dig 65 feet (20 meters)of tunnel in a single day.

Bulldozers

Aardvarks are peculiar-looking animals, and one of the world's fastest burrowers. They have long claws and powerful legs that they use to dig into soft soil. If an aardvark is scared, it can dig a burrow several feet long in less than 5 minutes.

15

⇨ *An African aardvark comes out of its hole just as the sun is going down. It hunts at night for ant and termite nests, and catches the insects with its long, sticky tongue.*

On the Run

Most land animals can crawl, walk, or run. Choosing the best way to travel may be the key to survival.

The **big cats** are famous for their elegant, fluid movements. They can move with either speed or stealth to hunt their prey.

Rapid runners

Cheetahs are the speed queens of the African plains. When a female has to find food to feed herself and her cubs, she needs to be fast and fearless to catch her prey. From a standing start, a cheetah can reach a record-breaking speed of more than 60 miles (96 kilometers) hour in just 3 seconds.

⇧ *Cheetahs can only run at top speed for about one minute. They get so hot when they run that they would die if they kept going.*

ACTUAL «« SIZE »»

Golden-rumped elephant shrew

9   6   5   4   3   2   1   in

Striped stalkers

Tigers use stealth rather than speed to hunt. They slowly stalk their prey, silently creeping up on an unsuspecting animal, such as a deer. They use speed only at the last minute, when they launch a sudden, deadly attack.

➡ *A tiger generally hunts alone. When it pounces on its prey, it can leap a distance of over 30 feet (5 to 10 meters).*

17

Elephant shrews can run across the forest floor at up to 15.5 miles (25 kilometers) per hour. A man would have to run at 2485 miles (4000 kilometers) per hour to achieve the same speed for his size!

Getting a Grip

Moving through the treetops needs good eyesight and a firm grip on the branches.

Animals that live in trees often have plenty of tasty fruit to hand. Being up high generally keeps the animals out of the reach of predators prowling below.

King of the swingers

Gibbons, monkeys, and chimps can leap and swing through trees, grabbing branches with their hands and feet. Monkeys even use their tails to grip onto branches. Gibbons, with their long arms and hooklike hands, are the fastest swingers of all.

⇧ *White-handed gibbons can grip onto thin branches using both their toes and fingers.*

Flying dragons

Lizards can't fly between trees, so some of them leap instead. Flying dragons are lizards that have wide flaps of skin that help them to glide.

⇦ *The shape of a flying dragon's body works like a parachute, slowing down the lizard as it falls.*

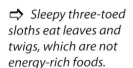 *Sleepy three-toed sloths eat leaves and twigs, which are not energy-rich foods.*

Slow sloths

Sloths rarely stir from their treetop homes. They hang upside down from branches and snooze for most of the day. Once a week, they slowly clamber down to the ground to **defecate** at a favorite spot. It takes them one whole minute to travel just 10 feet (3 meters).

19

The no. 1 leaping squirrel **RECORD BREAKER** is the ...

GIANT FLYING SQUIRREL

A giant flying squirrel, which has flaps of skin rather than wings, once leapt from a tree and soared for 1476 feet (450 meters) before landing safely.

Mini-Movers

Some little animals can move at great speed when they need to.

Others prefer to take life more slowly. Moving slowly is a good idea when you don't want to attract attention to yourself.

Red for danger

Bloody-nosed beetles can't fly, and they can't run quickly either. So instead of escaping from predators, they put them off by oozing a bright-red droplet of blood from their mouth.

⬆ *Stick insects mimic sticks, so they either stay very still or move extremely slowly.*

⬇ *Red spells danger in the animal kingdom, so when a bird sees a bloody-nosed beetle, it stays away.*

20

Take off!

Fleas are parasites, which means they feed off other living animals. Cat fleas can make giant leaps to get from one cat to another, to suck their blood. They have blocks of a rubber-like material in their legs that are squashed, then released, like tightly coiled springs.

➡ *A tiny cat flea can leap a distance of 13 inches (34 centimeters)—that's 170 times its own body length!*

21

ACTUAL ‹‹‹ SIZE ›››

Death's head hawkmoth

Hawkmoths can fly, in short bursts, at a top speed of 34 miles (54 kilometers) per hour. They twist and turn their wings in four different directions to get maximum lift and speed.

in   1   2   3   4

Slitherers

Animals that slither do not have limbs, such as legs and wings, to help them move.

Instead, slitherers rely on powerful muscles that work together to move their bodies along.

Deadly mamba

Black mambas are aggressive attackers. These snakes are among the most dangerous in the world. Their bite is deadly, and they can race over land faster than a person can run away.

22

The no. 1 longest worm **RECORD BREAKER** is the ...

BOOTLACE WORM

Worms have tiny bristles on their bodies that help them to slither over ground or the seabed. The longest worms of all are bootlace worms. They live in the North Sea and can measure 180 feet (55 meters) long.

⇐ *The black mamba's scales are smooth, not slimy. This helps the snake to slip over the ground at great speed.*

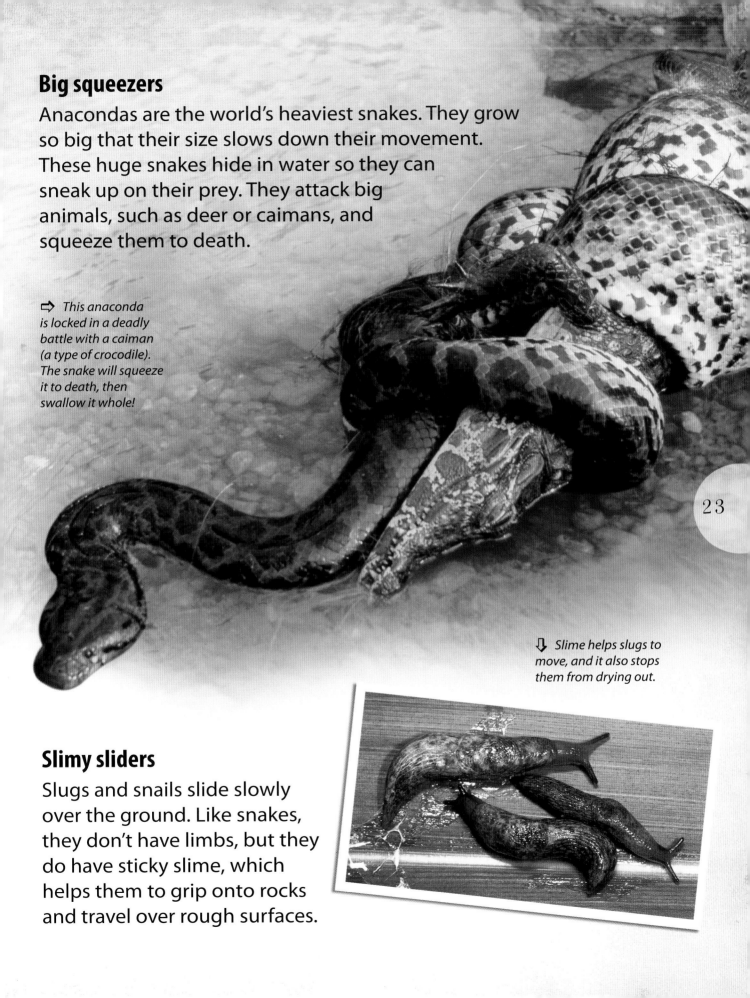

Big squeezers

Anacondas are the world's heaviest snakes. They grow so big that their size slows down their movement. These huge snakes hide in water so they can sneak up on their prey. They attack big animals, such as deer or caimans, and squeeze them to death.

⇨ *This anaconda is locked in a deadly battle with a caiman (a type of crocodile). The snake will squeeze it to death, then swallow it whole!*

23

⇩ *Slime helps slugs to move, and it also stops them from drying out.*

Slimy sliders

Slugs and snails slide slowly over the ground. Like snakes, they don't have limbs, but they do have sticky slime, which helps them to grip onto rocks and travel over rough surfaces.

Weird Walkers

Animals with long legs can usually run. Those with shorter legs are more likely to waddle, hop, or crawl.

Crocodiles and lizards have legs that are positioned to the sides of their bodies, rather than underneath. This means that their bodies appear to swing from side to side as they move. Despite the clumsy way they waddle, crocodiles can change from slow to speedy in an instant.

⇦ *Crocodiles warm up in the sun before returning to the water. Then they hide beneath the surface, watching for prey.*

⇨ *It takes a Californian desert tortoise a whole minute to walk just 10 feet (3 meters).*

⇩ *Centipedes need speed so they can catch small bugs to eat.*

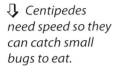

Slow and steady

Tortoises are famous for being slow. Their shells are so heavy that they can't take long or fast steps. Luckily, they do not need speed! They eat plants and stay safe from predators by hiding in their tough shell.

Lots of legs

Centipedes can quickly scamper under stones to avoid predators. They have many pairs of legs, which move in waves, starting from the animal's head and moving down its body.

ACTUAL «« SIZE »»

Ghost crabs hunt fast-moving sand fleas, so they depend on speed to eat and survive. They can scuttle over the sand at more than 4 miles (7 kilometers) per hour.

Ghost crab

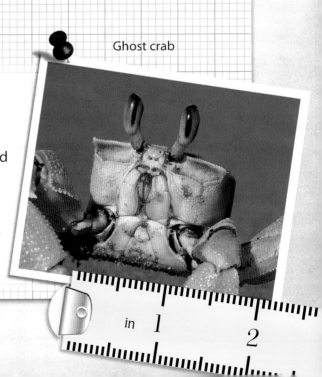

in 1   2

Energy Savers

Locomotion takes energy. Some underwater animals prefer to save energy either by staying still or by drifting through the water.

Creatures that live underwater have a big advantage over those that live on land. If they stay in one place, water currents bring food, such as tiny drifting animals and plants, straight to them.

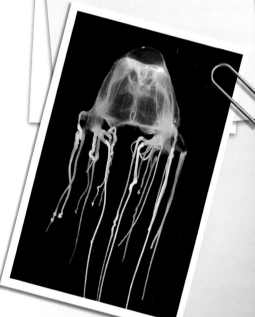

 ⇐ *Polyps have tiny stingers on their tentacles, which catch and sting small sea creatures.*

26

Waving tentacles

Small, soft **polyps** are animals that build stony cups, called coral, around themselves. Their **tentacles** poke out to catch animals floating past. Sea anemones are similar to coral polyps, but larger. They attach themselves to rocks with strong suckers.

Filter feeders

Shelled animals, such as mussels, suck seawater into their bodies and pass it over special filters to strain out any tiny particles of food. The water is pushed back to the sea, and the food is digested. This is called filter feeding.

⇐ Thousands of mussels grow together. They attach themselves to seaweed or rocks.

27

ACTUAL ‹‹‹ SIZE ›››

Christmas tree worms bury their bodies in the seabed, but their tree-like mouthparts stay in the water and trap small animals.

Christmas tree worm

in 1   2

Grow Slow

Speed is not just about how fast an animal moves. Animals can do other things at different speeds too, such as growing.

Incredible clams

Clams are slow-growing shelled animals that live at the bottom of the sea, filter feeding. They can live to be more than 400 years old. Deep-sea clams are possibly the slowest growers, taking 100 years to reach just 0.3 inches (8 millimeters) wide.

⇧ A blue whale baby swims alongside its mother. The baby adds about 200 pounds (90 kilograms) to its weight every day—that's the weight of an adult man!

⇦ Giant clams are the biggest shelled animals in the world. They can reach an amazing 5 feet (1.5 meters) wide.

Big babies

When a blue whale baby, or calf, is born, it already weighs about 3 tons. The baby then grows incredibly fast – about a thousand times faster than a human baby. Every day, it drinks more than 50 gallons (200 liters) of milk from its mother. The mother may lose a quarter of her own weight while raising her young.

ACTUAL ««« SIZE »»»

At nearly 10 inches (25 centimeters) long, the tadpole of the paradoxical frog grows much bigger than the adult frog—but no one knows why!

⇦ Half-grown tadpole

⇨ Paradoxical frog

in 1 2 3 4 5 6 7 8

Glossary

Big cat A large member of the cat family, such as a lion, tiger, cheetah or leopard.

Current A river of water that moves within an ocean or sea is called a current.

Defecate When an animal defecates, it gets rid of its solid waste, or feces.

Habitat The place where an animal or plant lives.

Insect A small animal with six legs, three body parts and a tough, shell-like outer covering.

Mammal An animal that has hair or fur, and feeds its young with milk. Mammals include people, dogs, bats and whales.

Mimic To copy or to pretend to be like something else.

Muscles The parts of the body that are attached to bones and help make the body move.

Polyp A soft-bodied sea creature with a tube-shaped body and a mouth surrounded by tentacles. When polyps live together in large groups, they form coral.

Predator An animal that hunts another animal to eat is a predator. A predator preys on other animals.

Prey An animal that is hunted for food is a prey animal.

Species A particular type of animal or plant is called a species.

Tentacle Some animals have long, bendy limbs, called tentacles, that they use for feeding, moving or feeling.

Thermal A current or column of warm air that rises upward in the sky is called a thermal.

Venom Some animals use a type of poison, called venom, to stun or kill other animals.

Warren An animal home made from holes connected to each other by tunnels is a warren. Rabbits and hares live in warrens.

Index

Notes for Parents and Teachers

Here are some ideas for activities that adults and children can do together.

◆ Speed is determined by two factors: distance and time. Help children to set out two markers, some distance apart, and measure that distance. Use a stopwatch to help them discover the time they take to cover the distance, and their speed. When they cover a longer distance, does their speed reduce or increase?

◆ Visit an aquarium to watch how fish and other aquatic animals are able to move in water. Talk about the shape of fast-swimming fish, and how being streamlined reduces water resistance.

◆ Use the Internet to help children find and watch videos of hummingbirds and peregrine falcons in flight.

◆ Explore human locomotion. Help children to find their muscles, and explain how the muscles contract and extend as they move our limbs. Talk about the different ways we can move, from crawling and climbing to swimming, and, if possible, try doing them all.

The publishers cannot accept liability for any information or links found on third-party websites.

32